My Number Book

Name

zero

one

two

three

four

five

six

seven

eight

nine

Number Tracing

Print, Laminate & Trace

Number Tracing

Print, Laminate & Trace

Name: _______

Number Tracing

Print, Laminate & Trace

Number Tracing

Print, Laminate & Trace

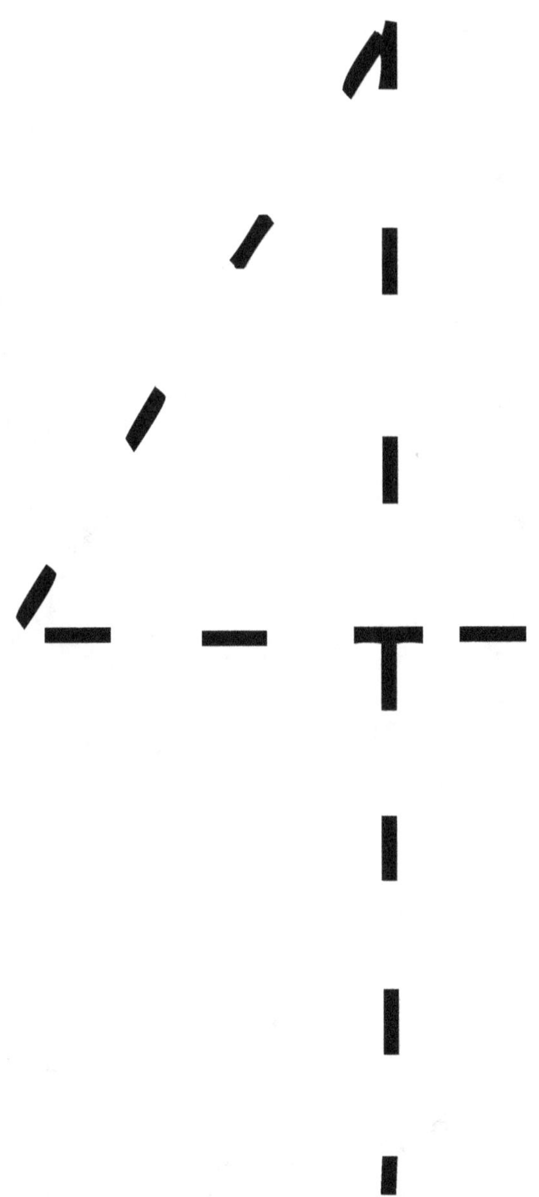

Number Tracing

Print, Laminate & Trace

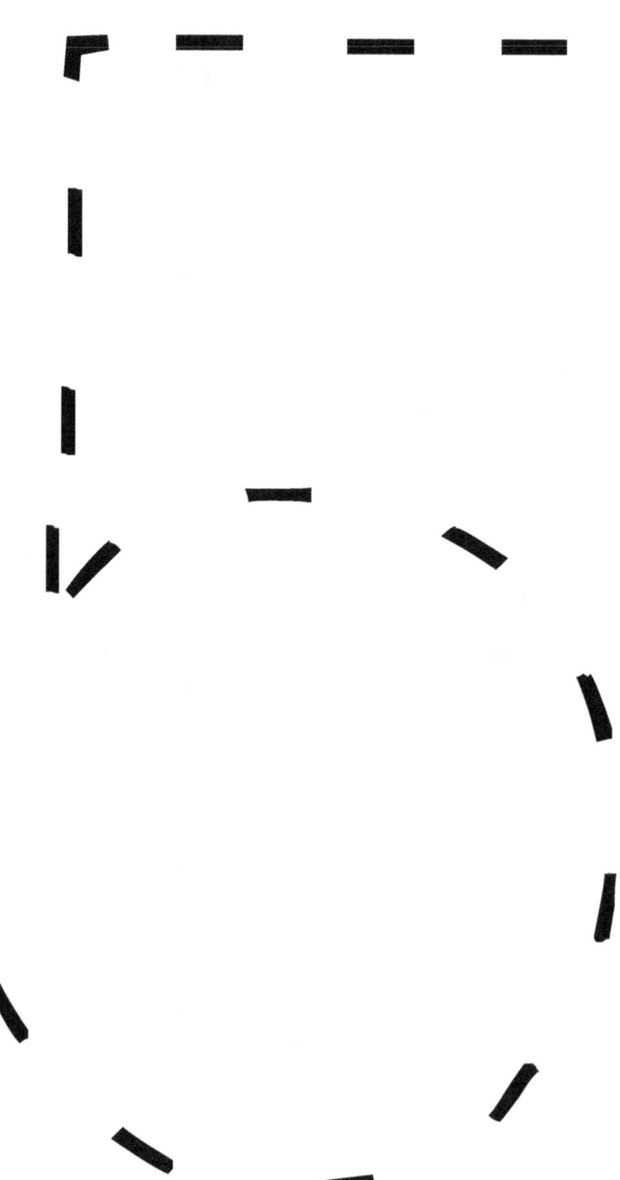

Number Tracing

Print, Laminate & Trace

Number Tracing

Print, Laminate & Trace

Name: __________

Number Tracing

Print, Laminate & Trace

Name: __________

Number Tracing

Print, Laminate & Trace

Number Tracing

Print, Laminate & Trace

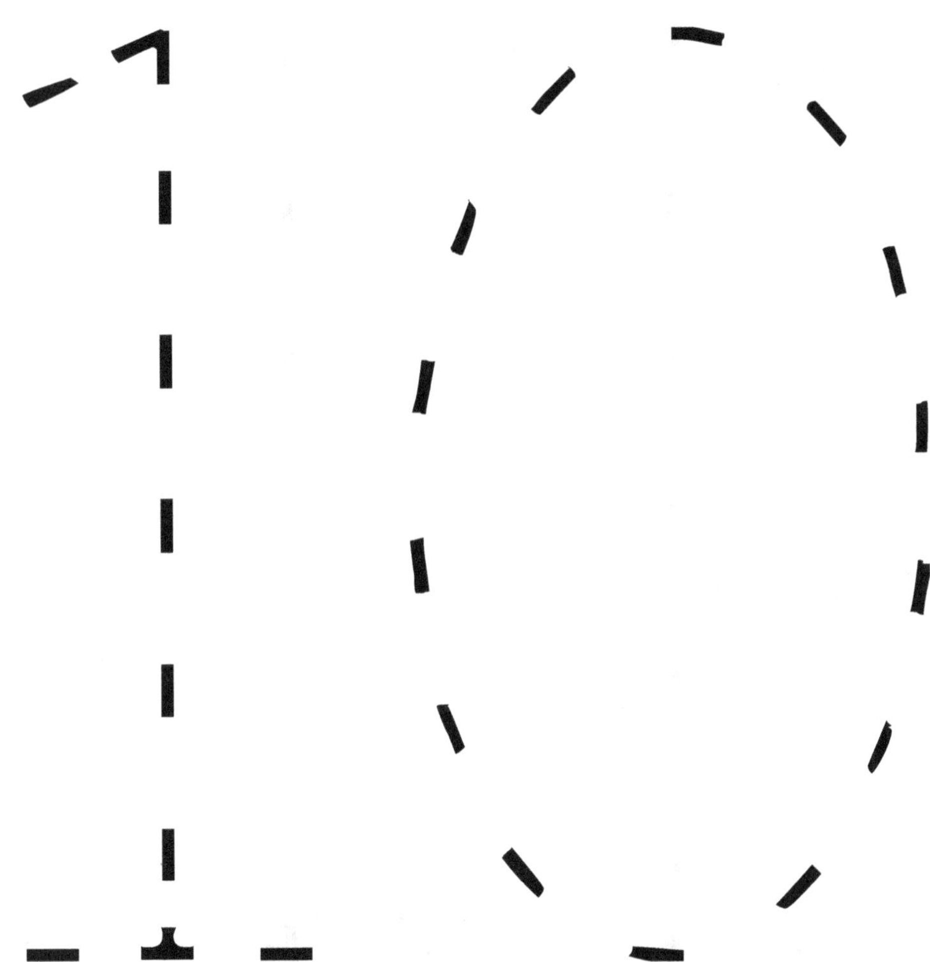

Name: _________

Number Tracing

Print, Laminate & Trace

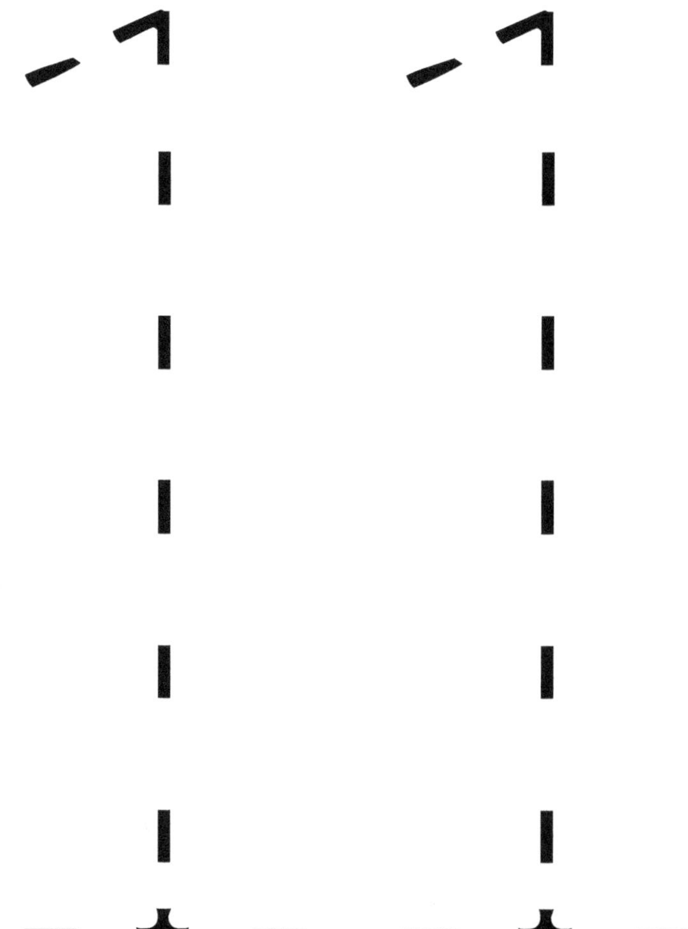

Number Tracing

Print, Laminate & Trace

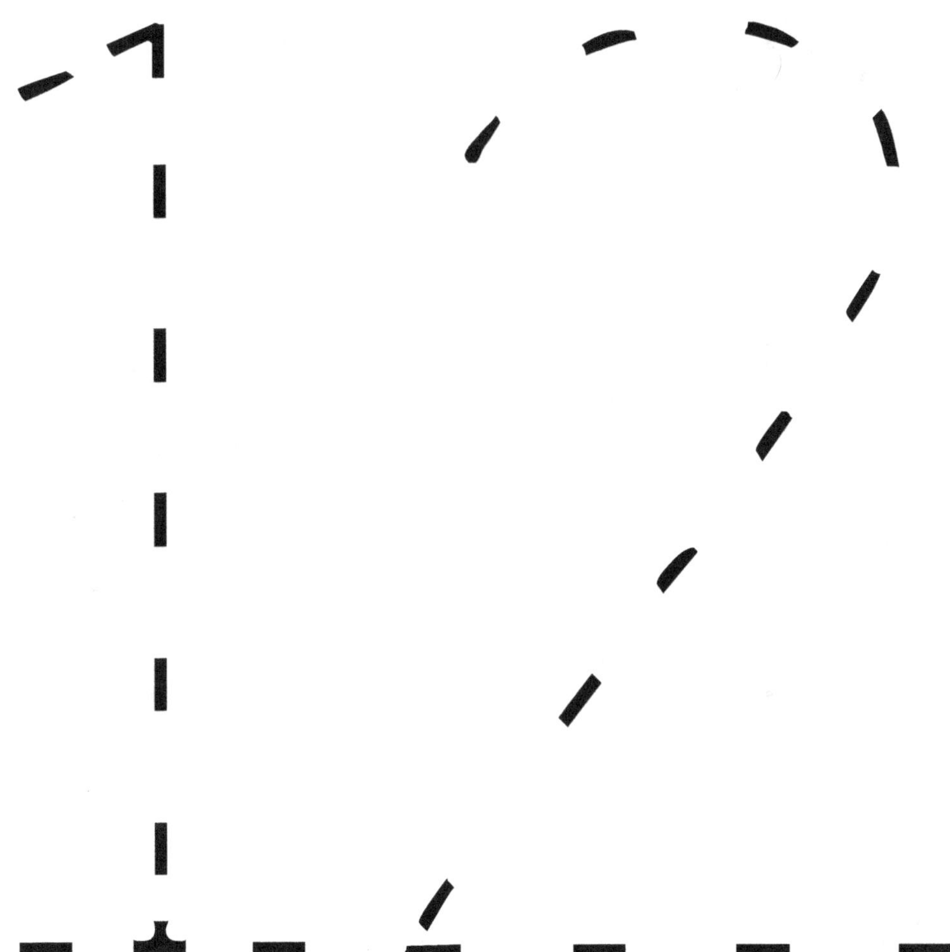

Number Tracing

Print, Laminate & Trace

Number Tracing

Print, Laminate & Trace

Number Tracing

Print, Laminate & Trace

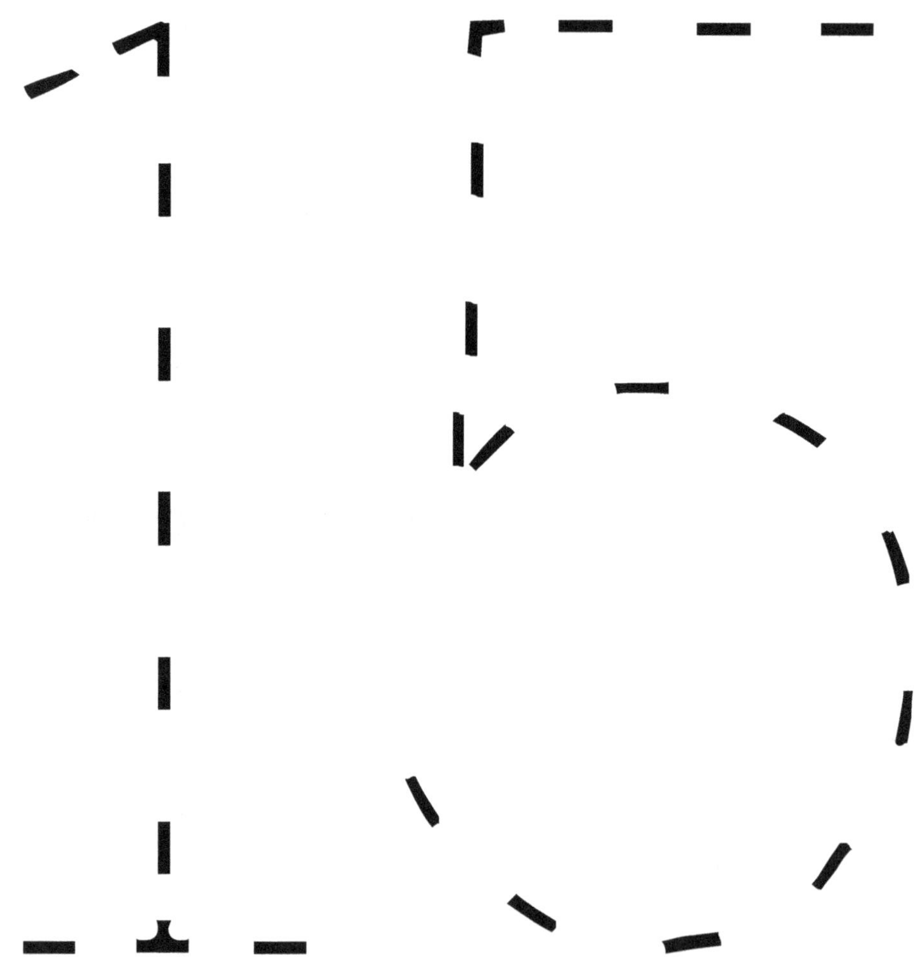

Number Tracing

Print, Laminate & Trace

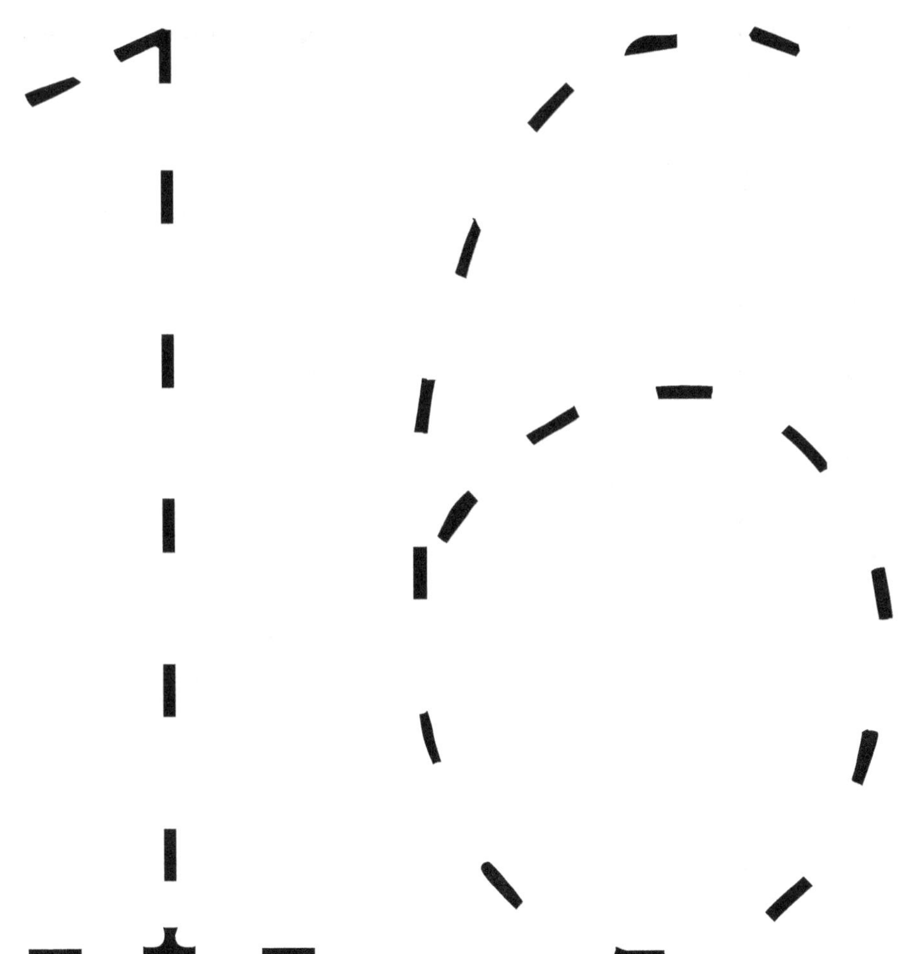

Name: _______________

Number Tracing

Print, Laminate & Trace

Number Tracing

Print, Laminate & Trace

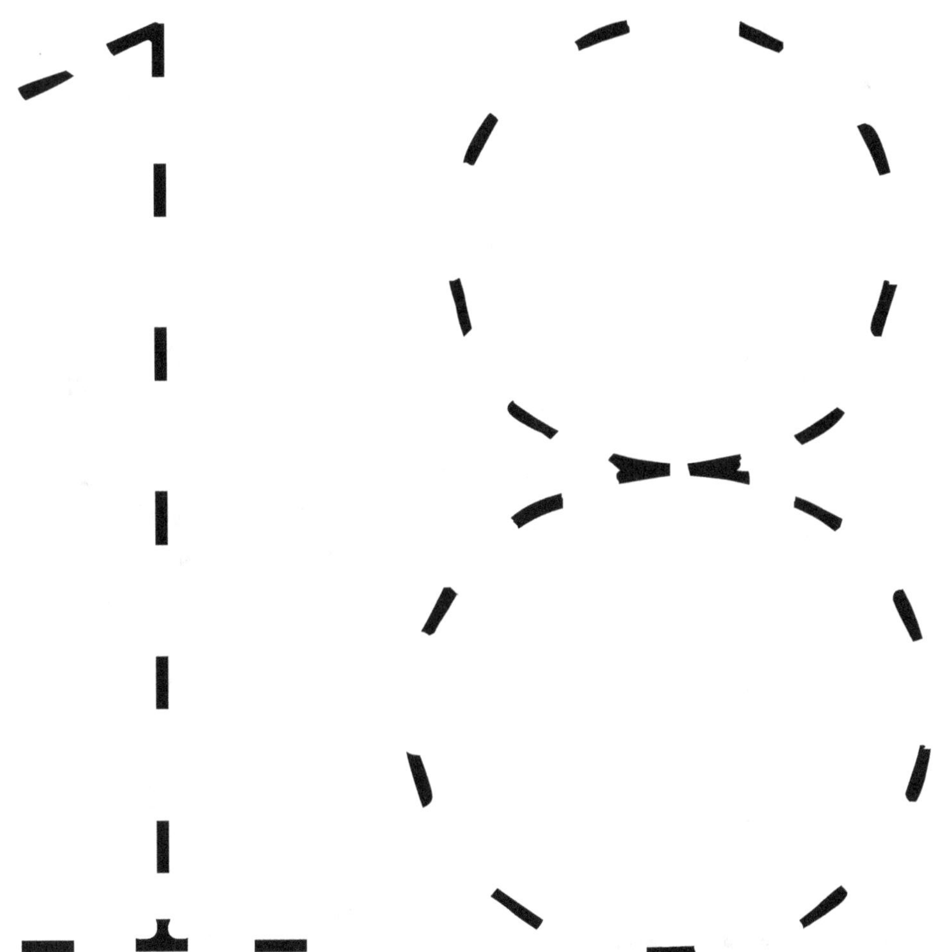

Number Tracing

Print, Laminate & Trace

Number Tracing

Print, Laminate & Trace

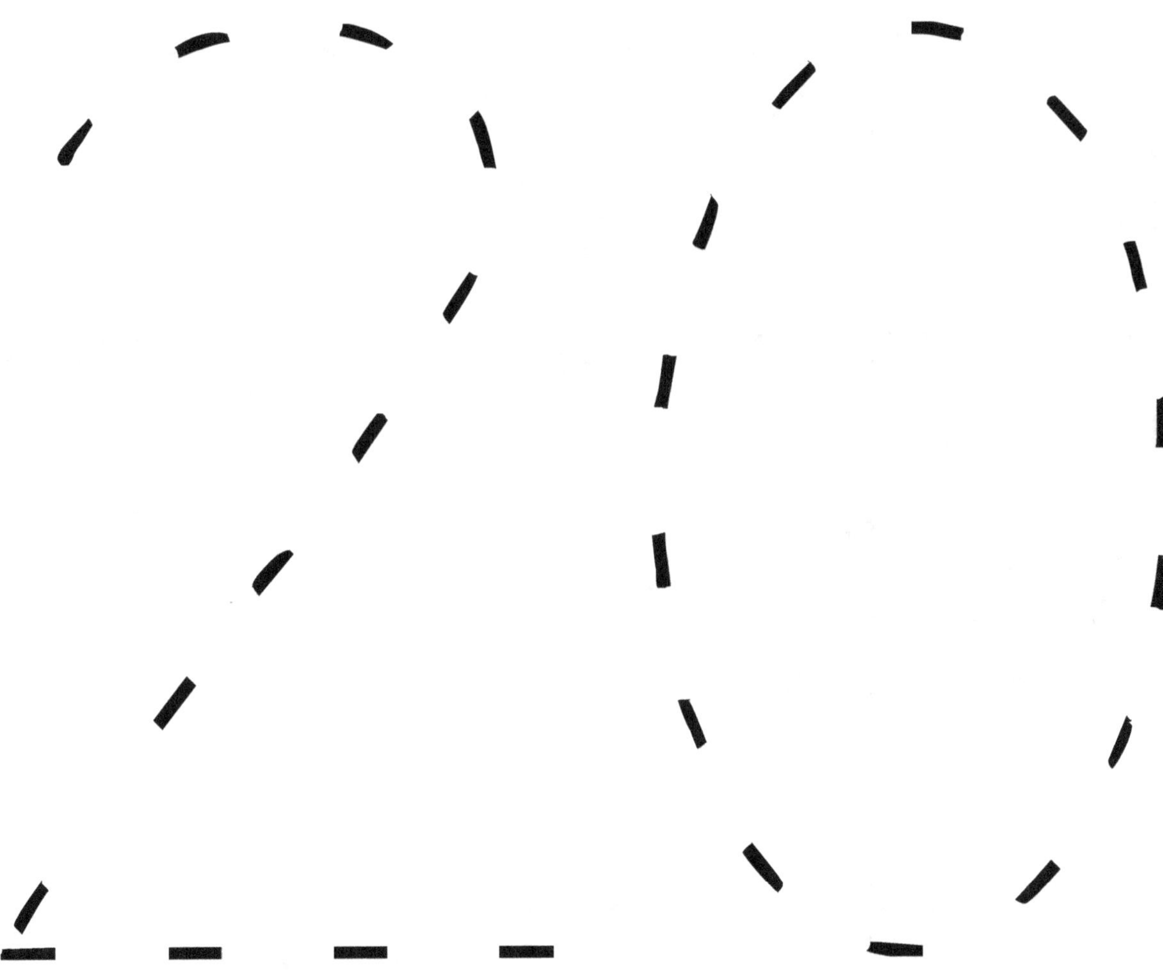

TRACING
NUMBERS

TRACE N° 1 & COUNT THE CAT

TRACE N° 2 & COUNT THE CATS

TRACING
NUMBERS

TRACE N° 3 & COUNT THE CATS

TRACING

NUMBERS

TRACE N° 4 & COUNT THE CATS

TRACING
NUMBERS

TRACE N° 5 & COUNT THE CATS

TRACING
NUMBERS

TRACE N° 6 & COUNT THE CATS

TRACING
NUMBERS

TRACE N° 7 & COUNT THE CATS

TRACING
NUMBERS

TRACE N° 8 & COUNT THE CATS

TRACING
NUMBERS

TRACE N° 9 & COUNT THE CATS

DIRECTIONS: TRACE THE WORDS AND NUMBERS BELOW.

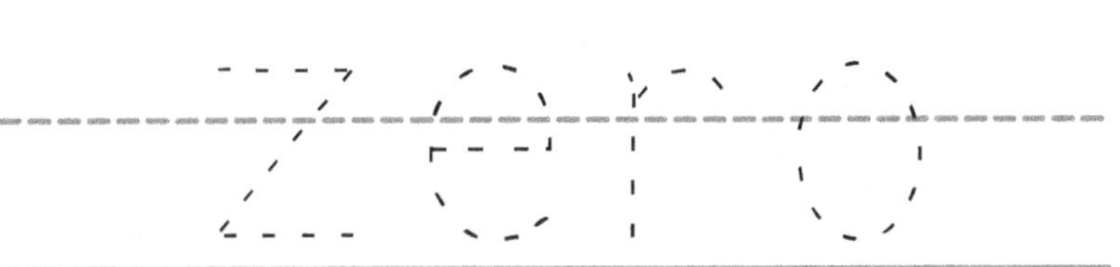

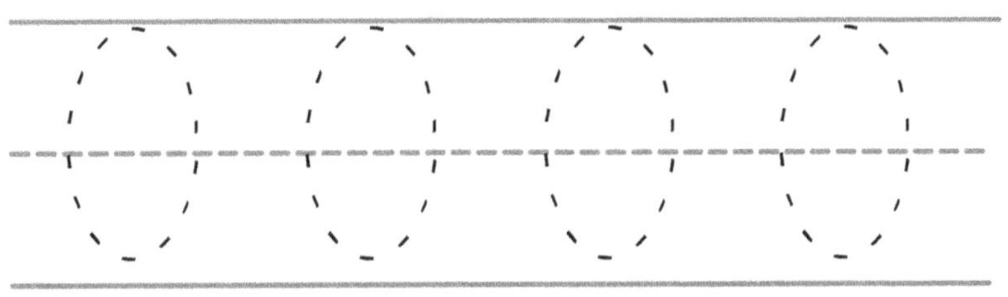

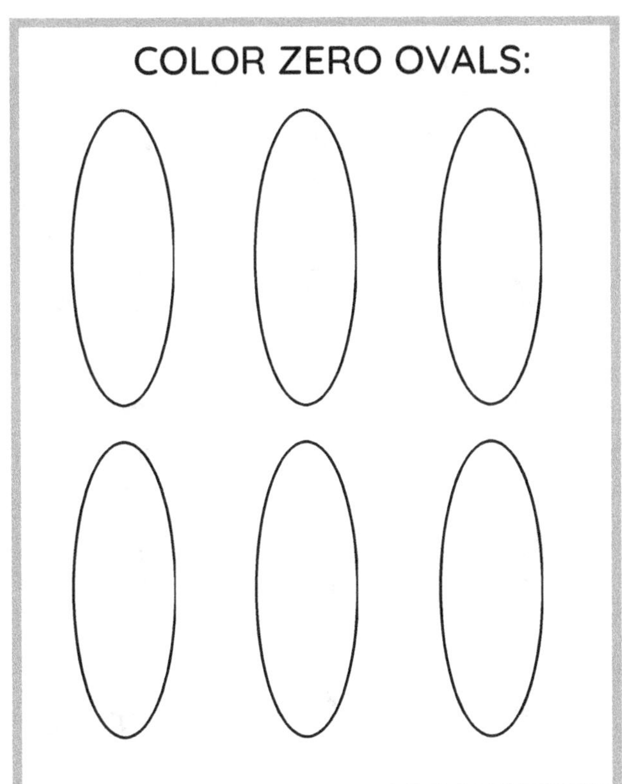

CIRCLE THE ZEROES:

5	0	3
1	0	2
0	5	4
4	0	6
0	6	1

DIRECTIONS: TRACE THE WORDS AND NUMBERS BELOW.

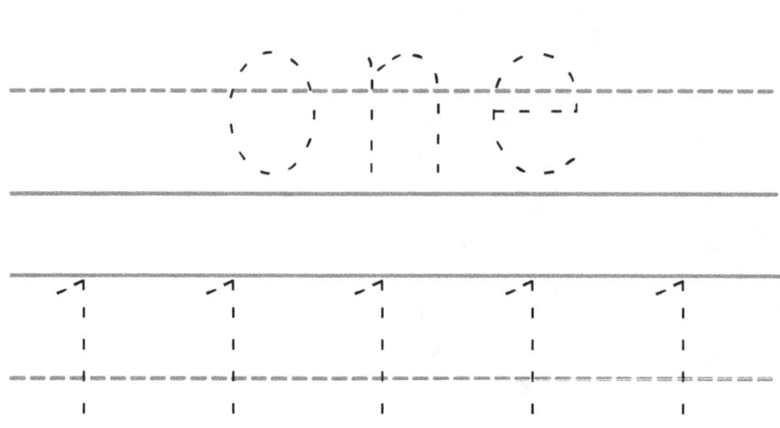

CIRCLE THE ONES:

1	3	5
4	2	1
6	1	8
1	7	1
2	1	4

Name: _______________________

DIRECTIONS: TRACE THE WORDS AND NUMBERS BELOW.

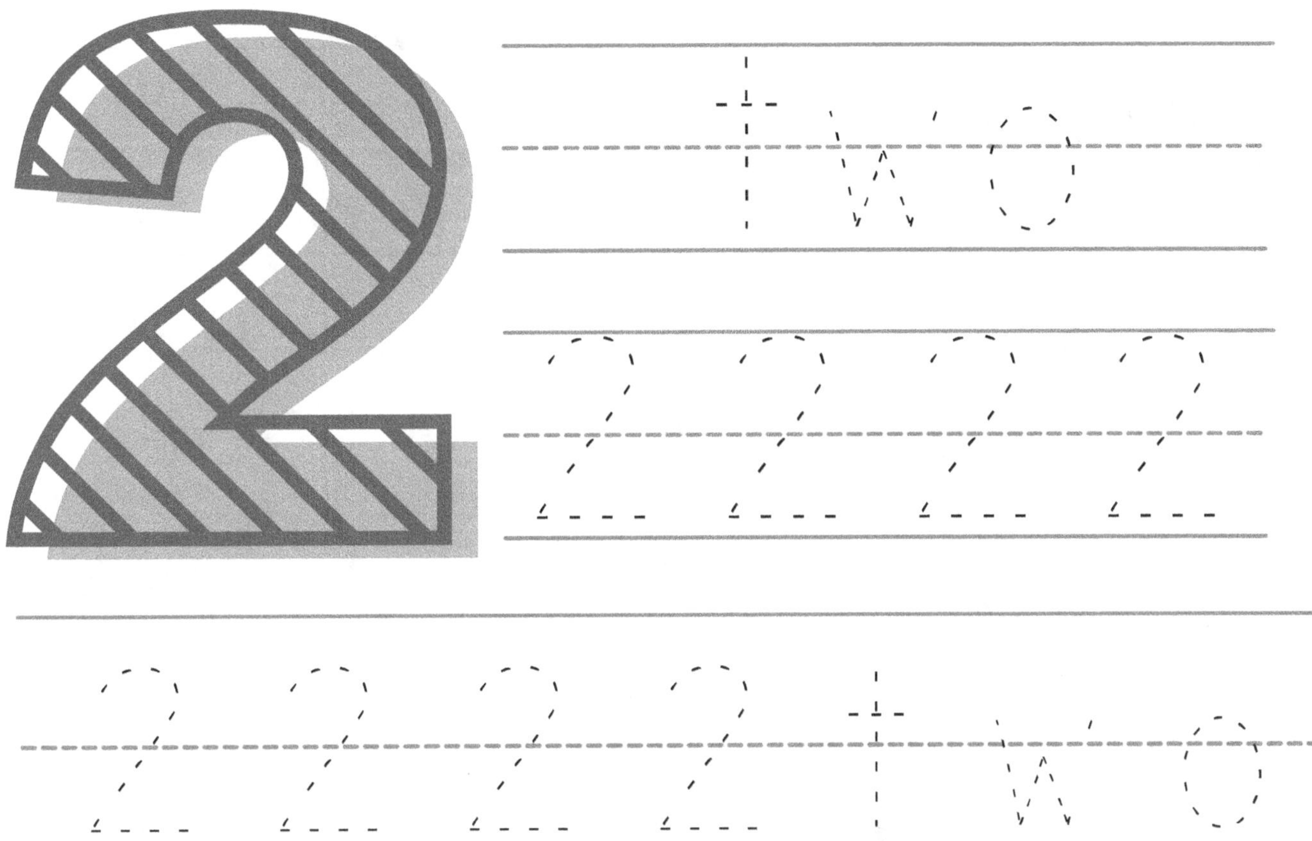

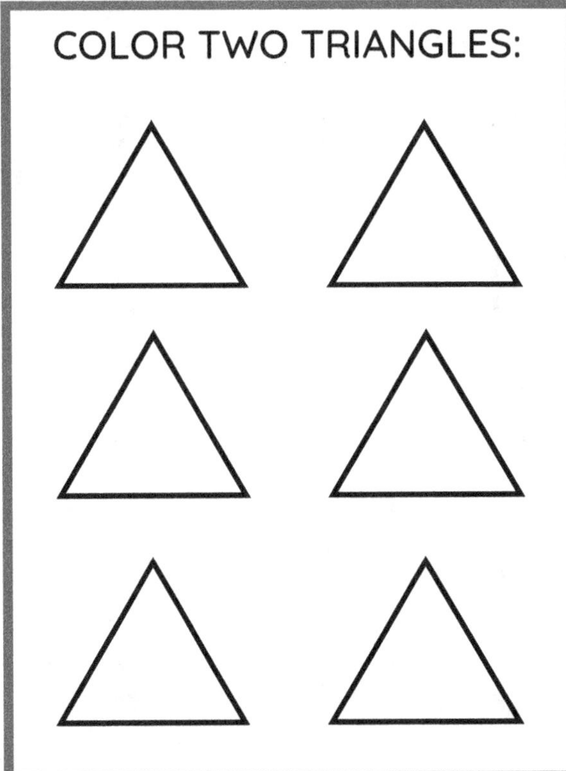

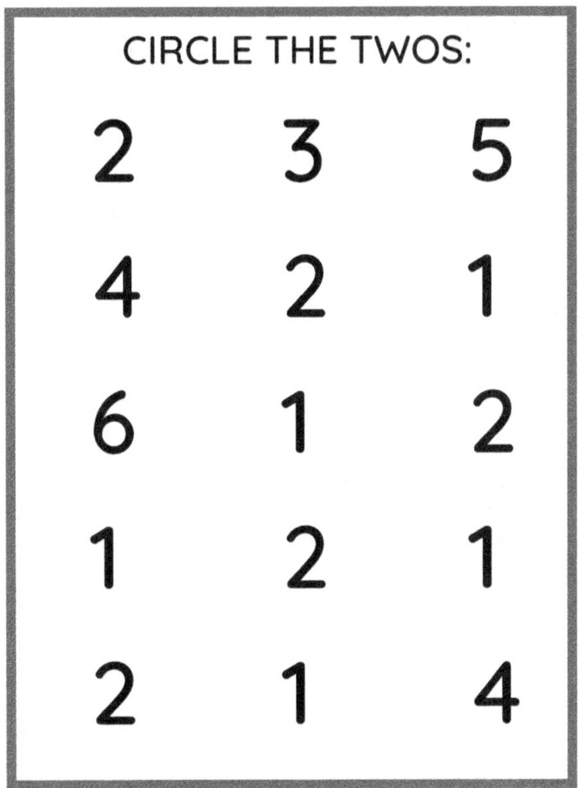

DIRECTIONS: TRACE THE WORDS AND NUMBERS BELOW.

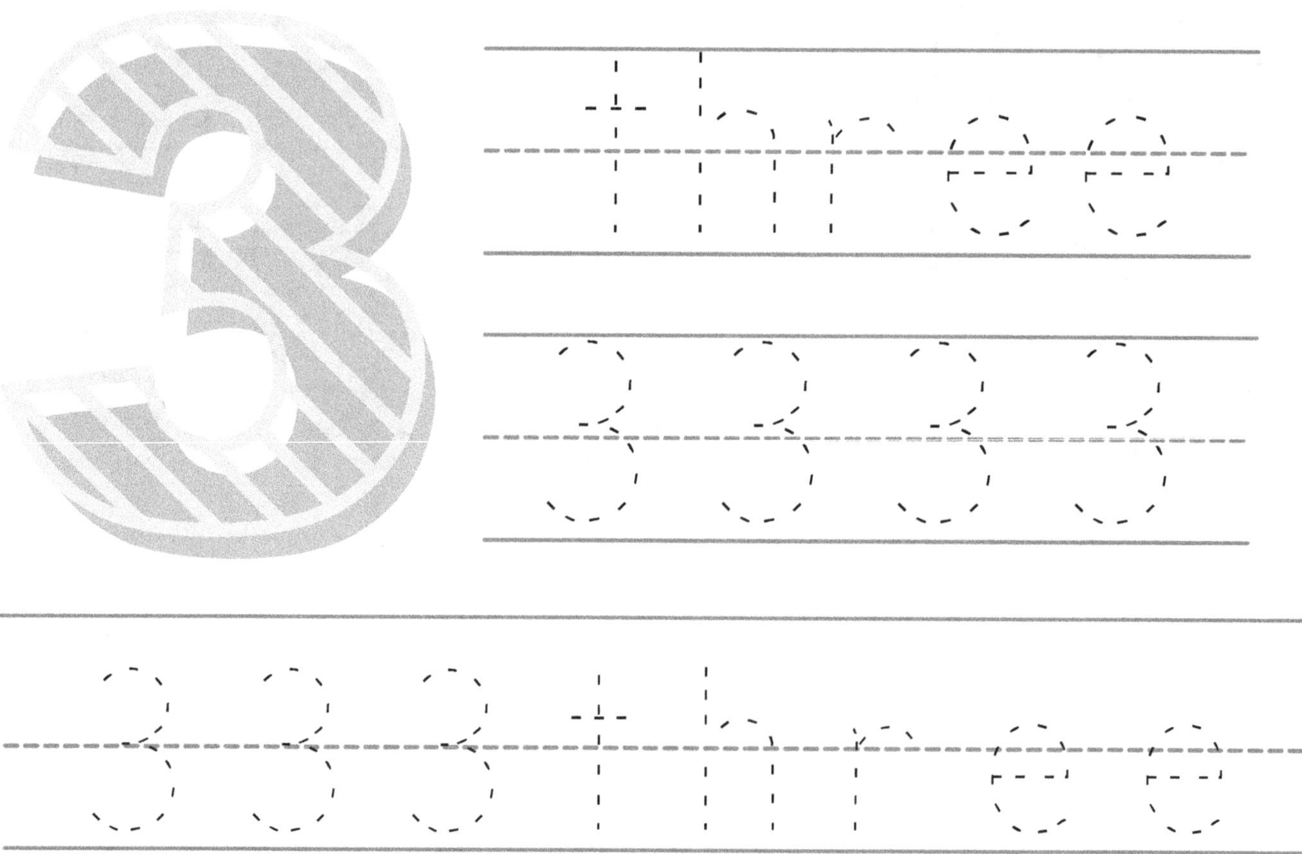

COLOR THREE SQUARES:

CIRCLE THE THREES:

2	3	5
4	2	3
3	1	2
3	5	1
6	3	4

DIRECTIONS: TRACE THE WORDS AND NUMBERS BELOW.

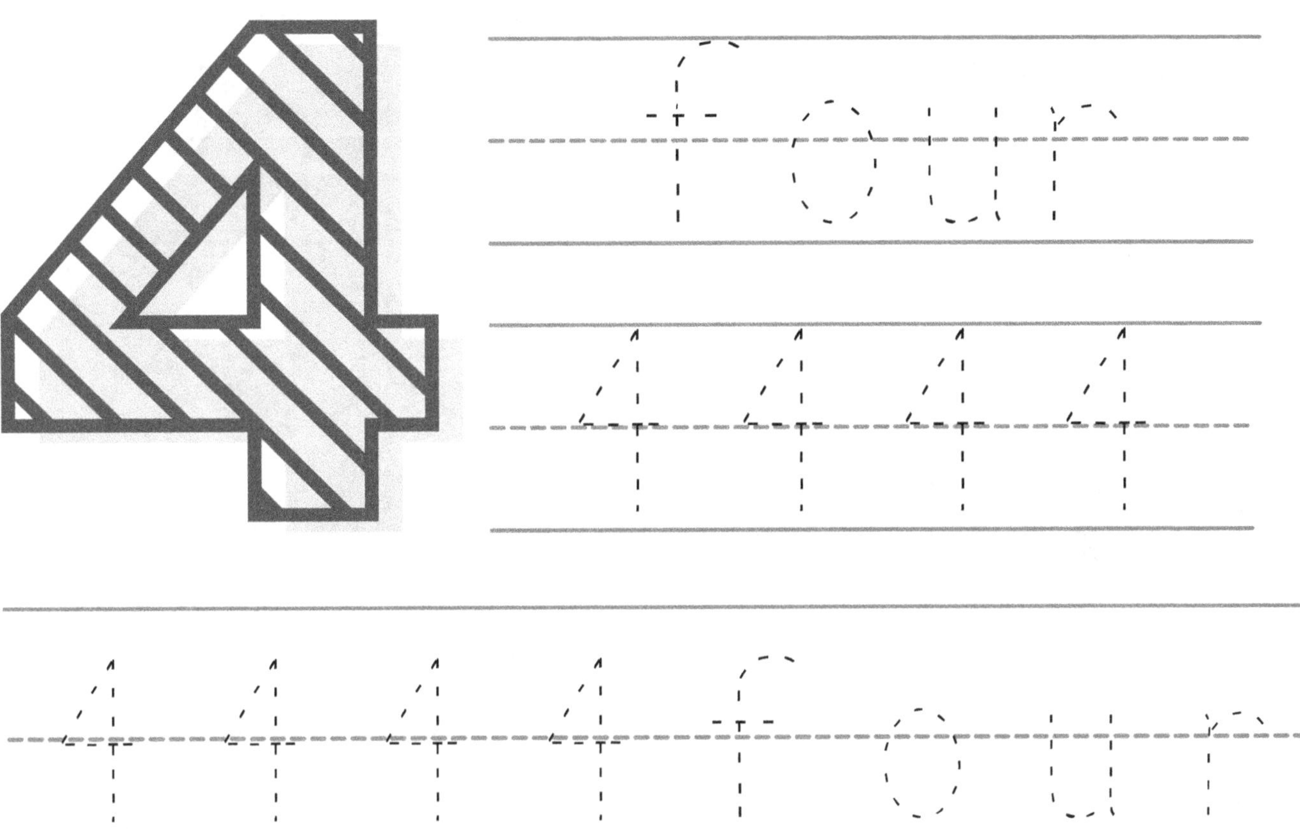

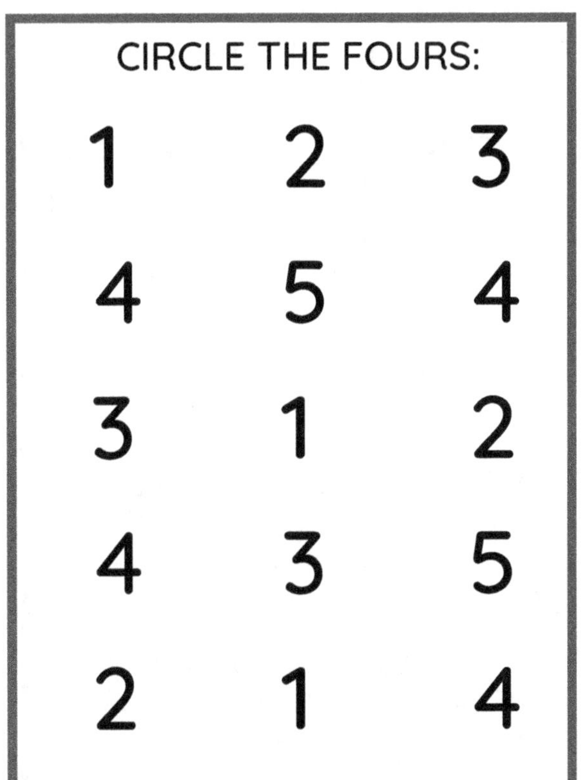

DIRECTIONS: TRACE THE WORDS AND NUMBERS BELOW.

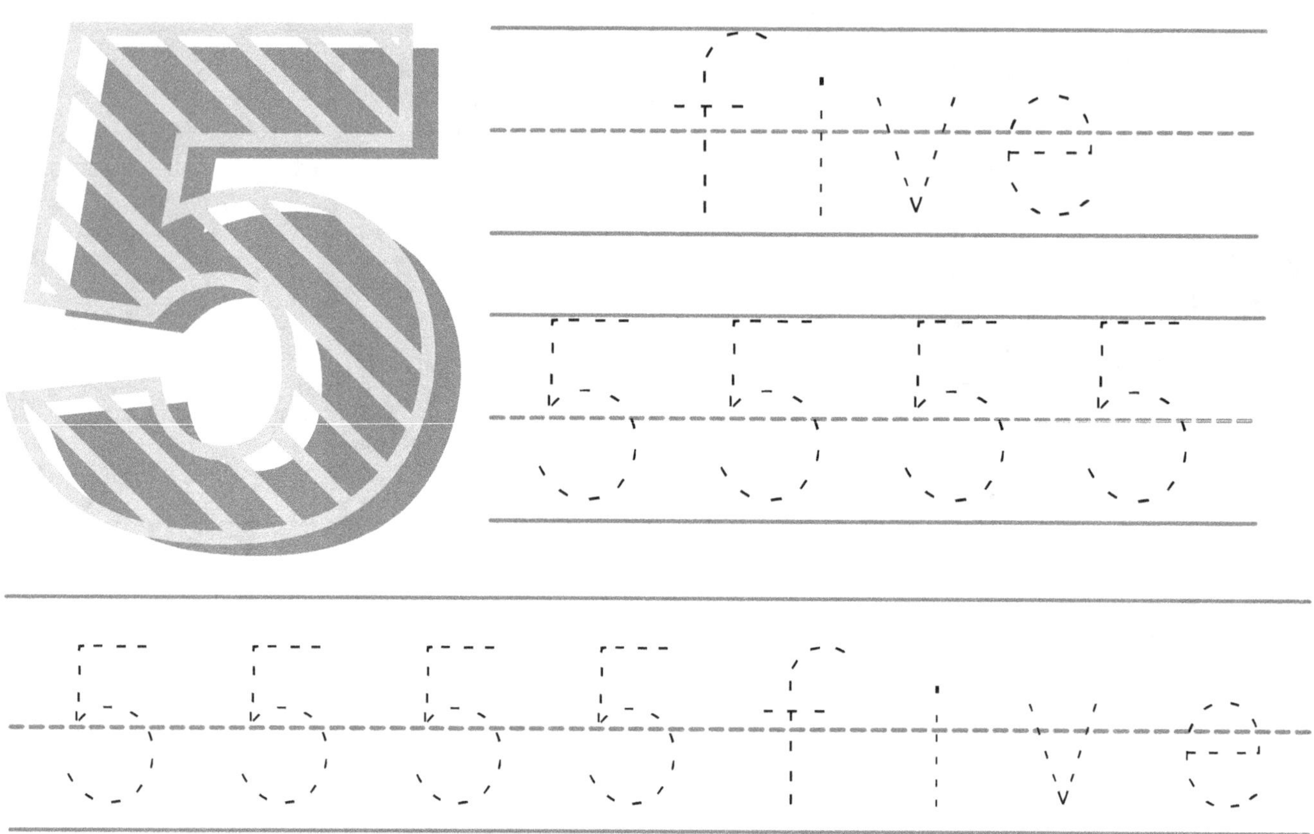

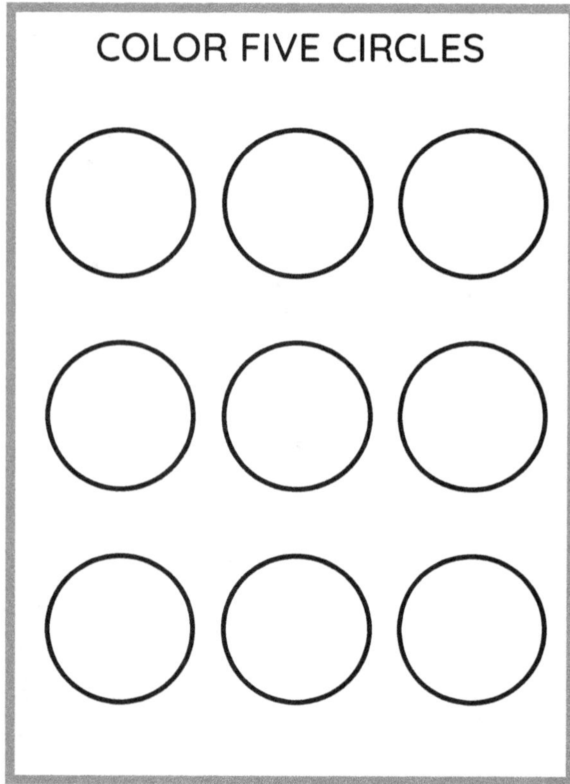

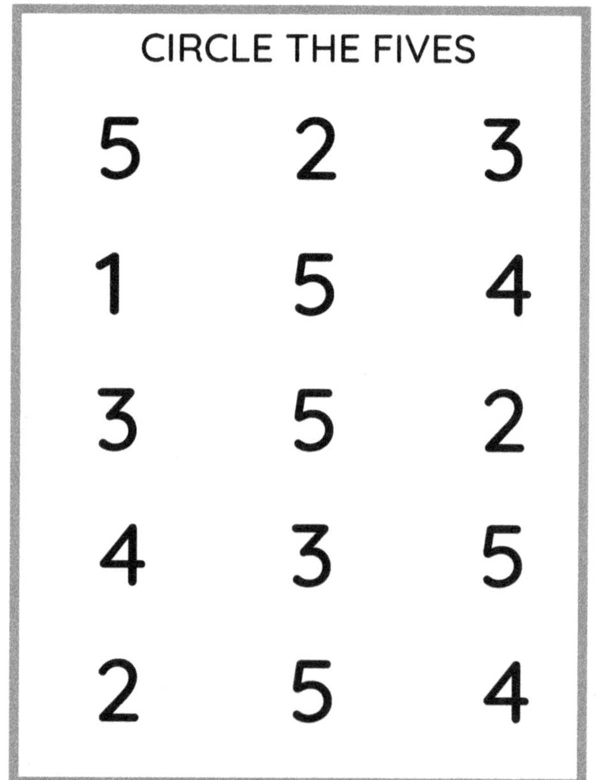

DIRECTIONS: TRACE THE WORDS AND NUMBERS BELOW.

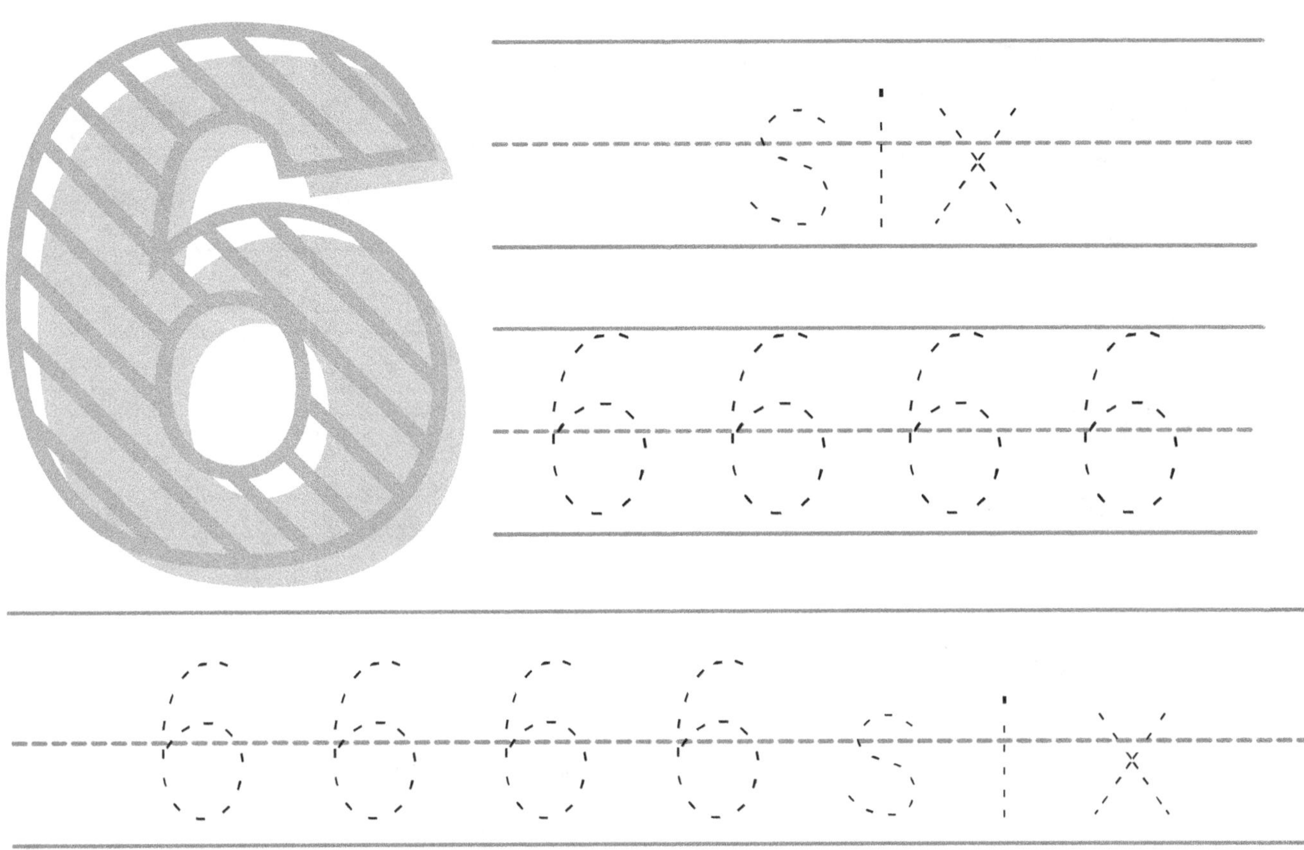

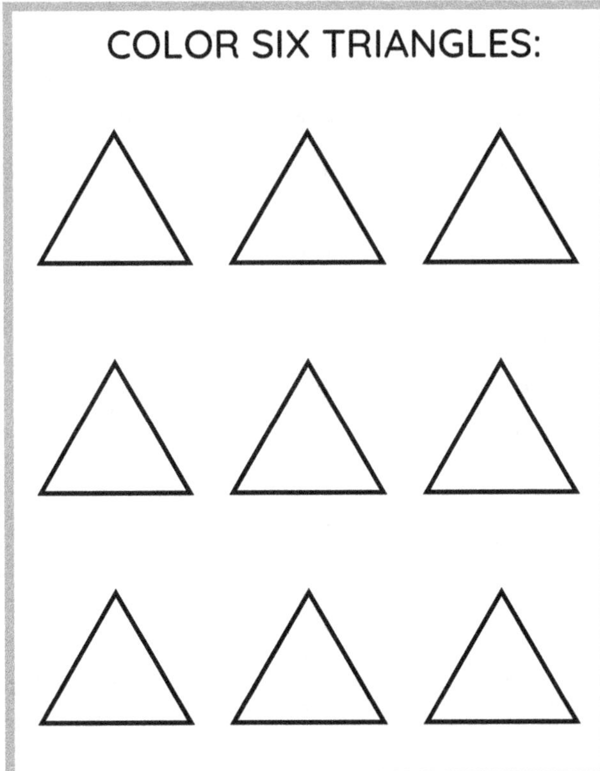

COLOR SIX TRIANGLES:

CIRCLE THE SIXES

5	6	3
1	2	6
6	5	4
4	3	6
2	6	1

DIRECTIONS: TRACE THE WORDS AND NUMBERS BELOW.

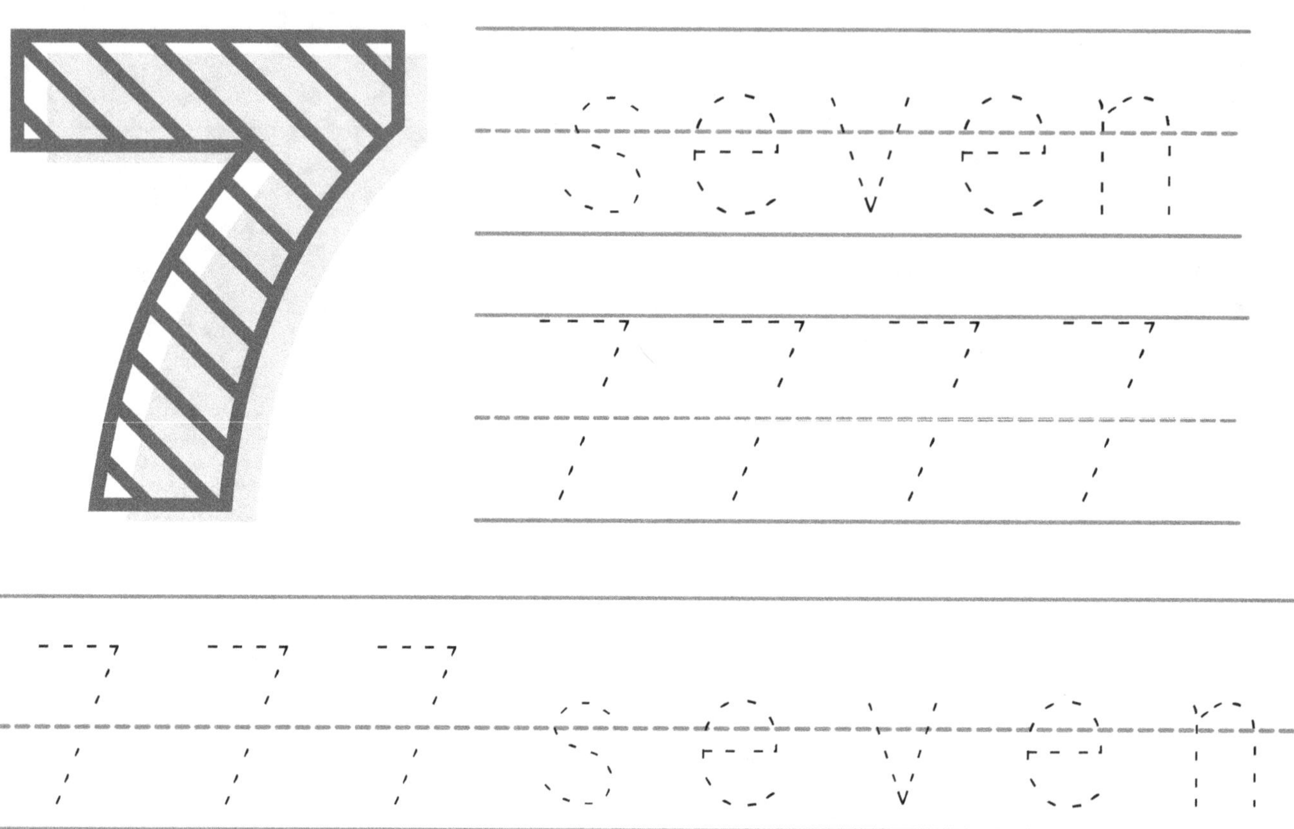

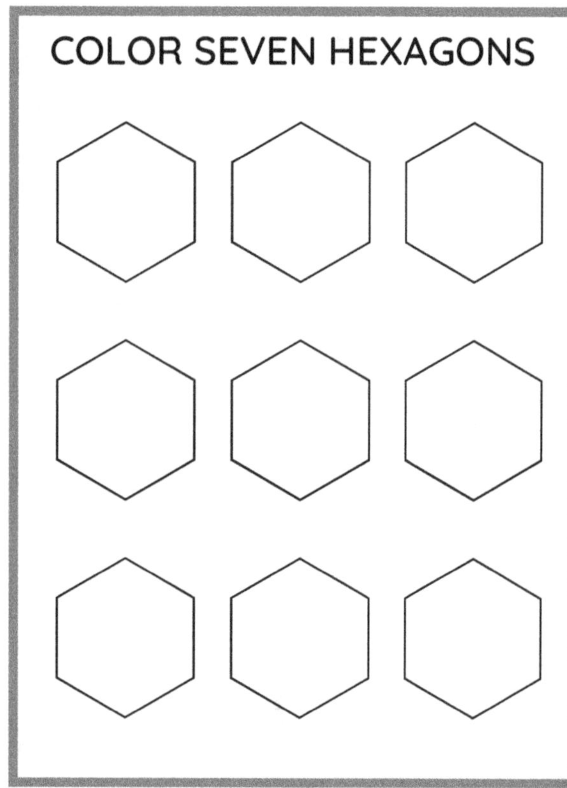

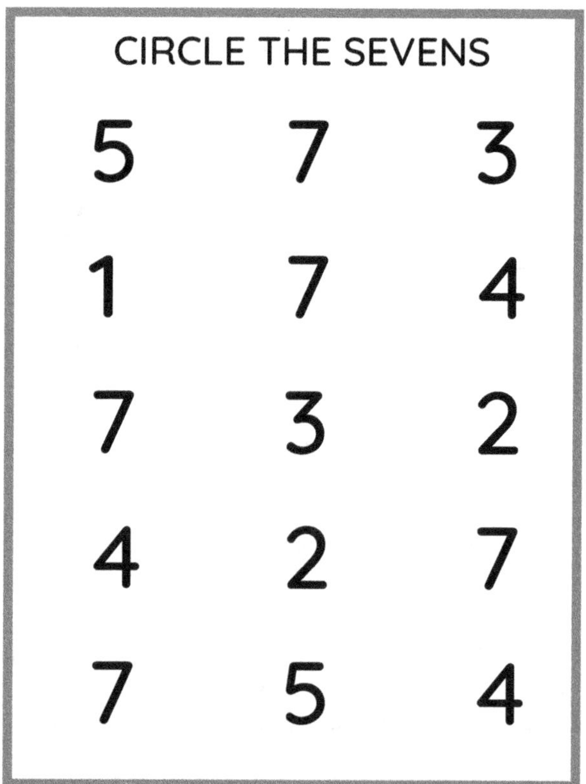

DIRECTIONS: TRACE THE WORDS AND NUMBERS BELOW.

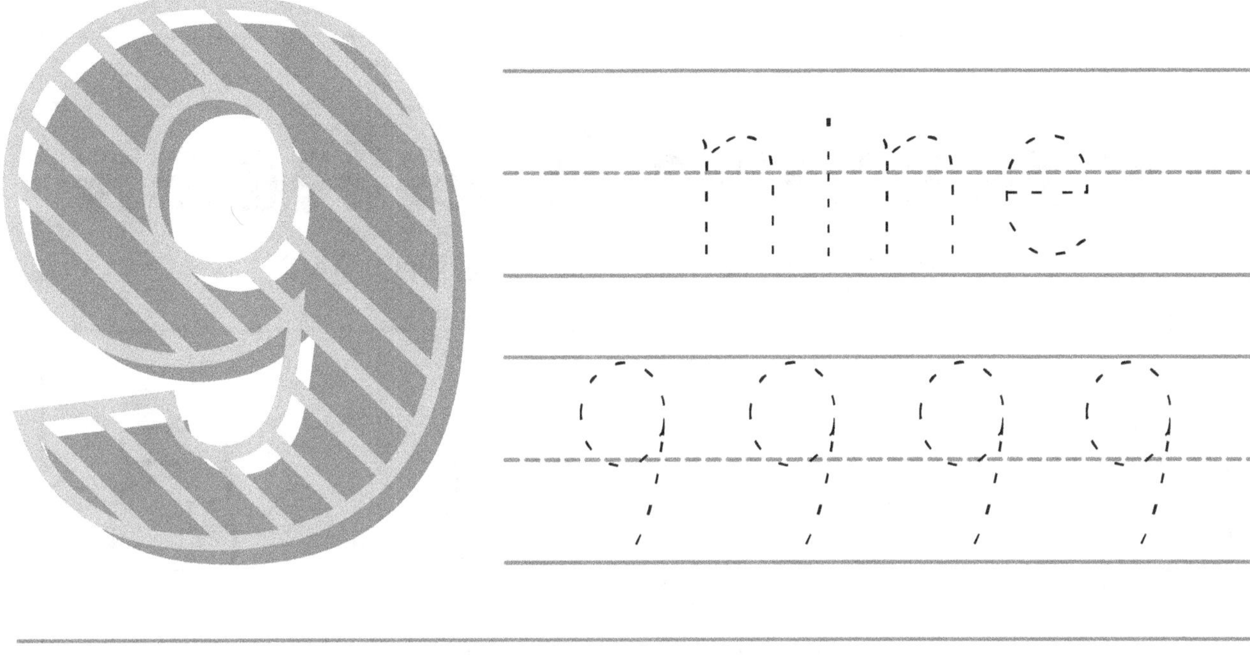

CIRCLE THE NINES:

9	8	6
4	7	9
8	6	9
4	9	8
9	5	1

Name:

Section:

Date:

Teacher:

Number Values

Color the number that has the bigger value

GREATER OR LESS THAN

Compare the numbers and write <, >, or =

10 ◯ 8	1  10
6 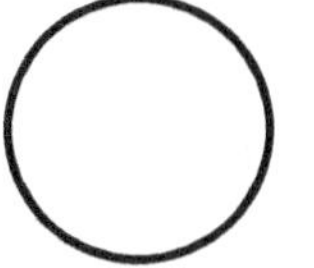 7	3  3
5 ◯ 5	0 ◯ 8
3 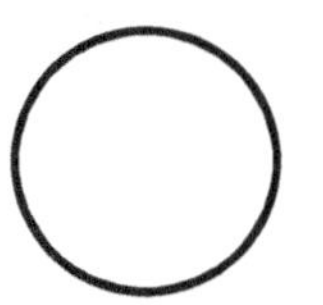 9	7 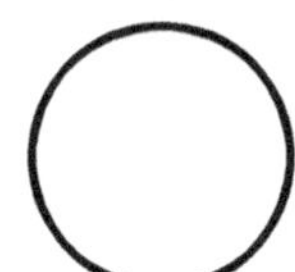 9
4 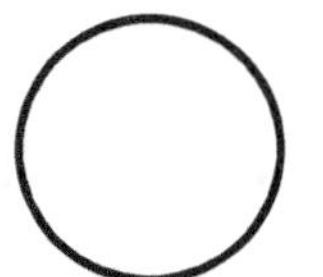 2	6 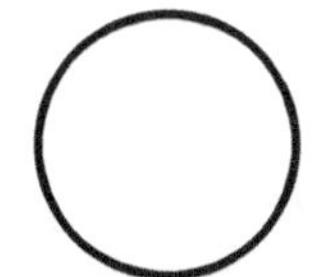 4

Name ___________________   Date ___________________

Before and After

Write the numbers that come before
and after the number in the middle.

8	**9**	10		**7**	
	6			**11**	
	3			**3**	
	5			**5**	
	12			**4**	
	18			**2**	

DIRECTIONS: TRACE THE NUMBERS IN THE CUPCAKES. IF TIME PERMITS, COLOR THE CUPCAKES.

TRACE THE NUMBERS

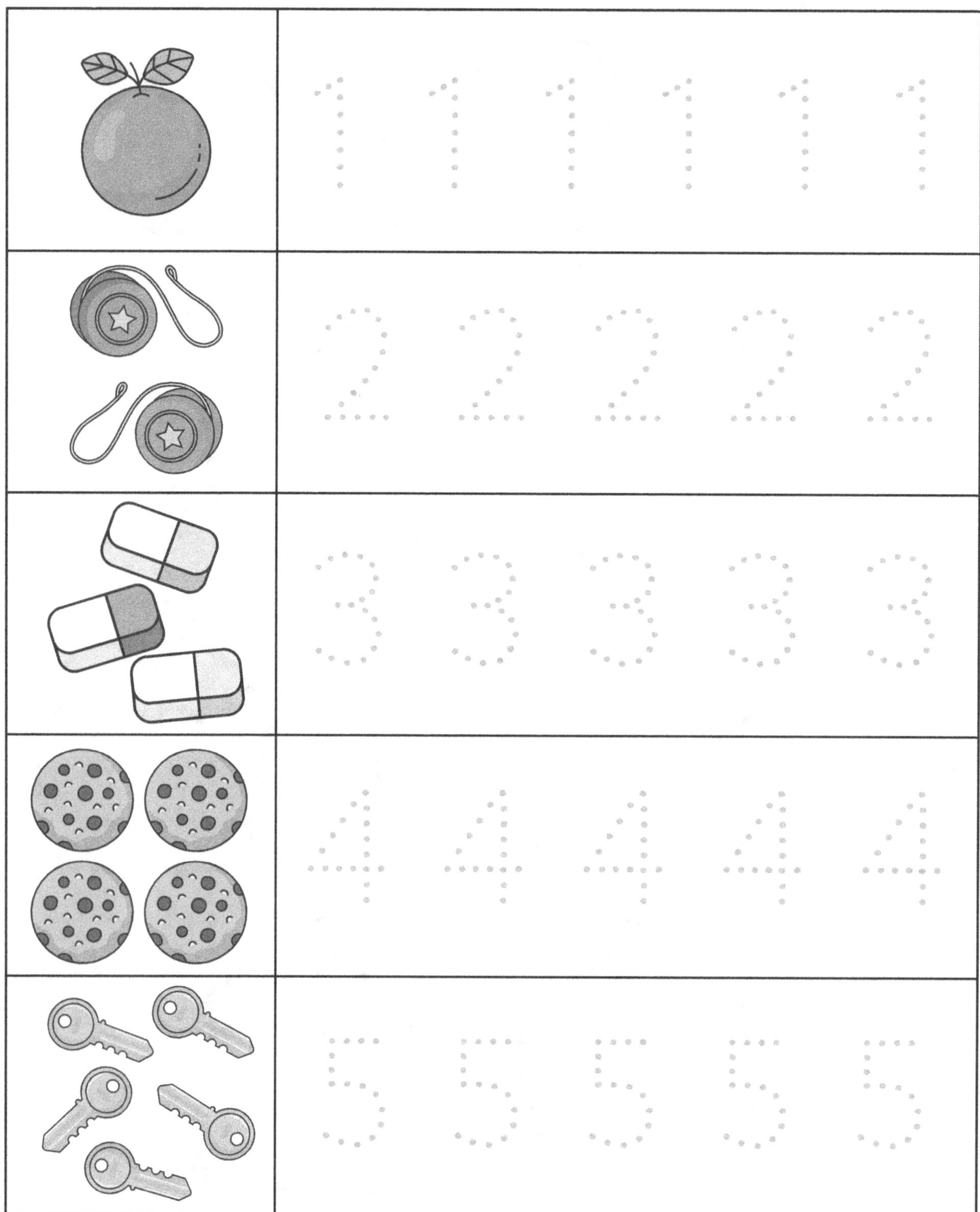

Name: _______________   Sect on: _______________

Teacher: _______________   Date: _______________

TRACING NUMBERS

Trace the numbers n the boxes.

1	1	1	1	1
2	2	2	2	2
3	3	3	3	3
4	4	4	4	4
5	5	5	5	5

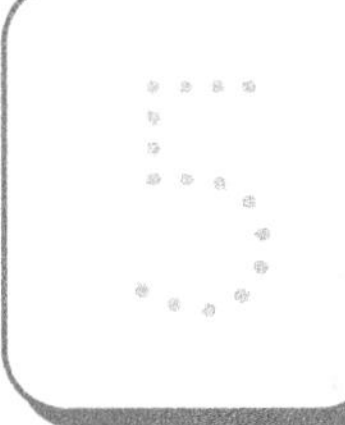
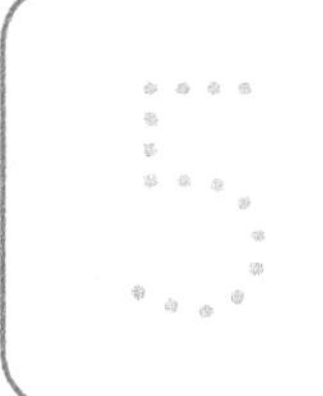

DIRECTIONS: USING BLACK, PRACTICE YOUR NUMBER WRITING. WHEN FINISHED COLOR THE EASTER EGGS.

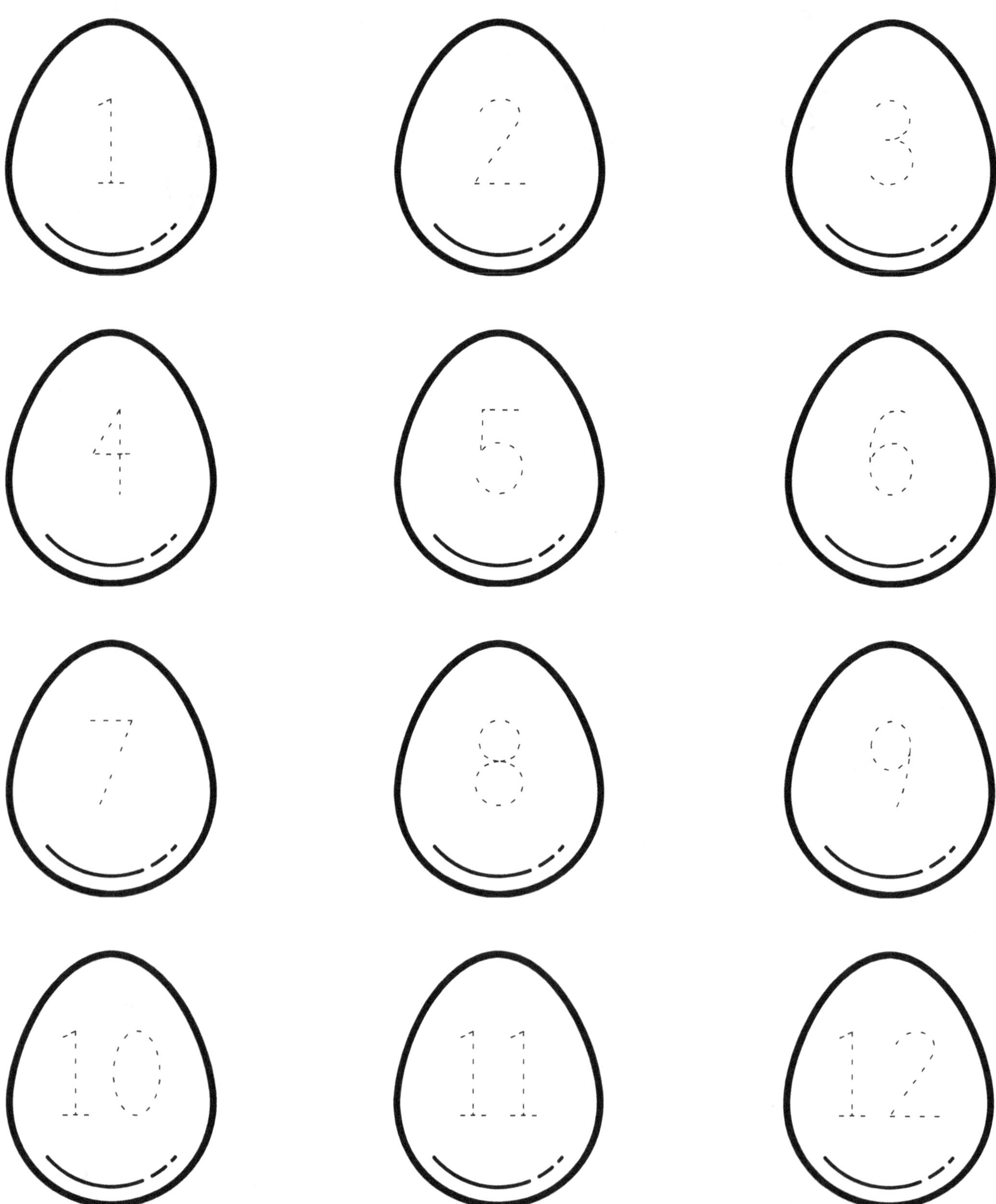

D rect ons: Help Cup d put the hearts n numer cal order from 1 to 10. Draw a l ne from heart to heart, Cup d got t started for you by draw ng a l ne between 1 and 2.

5

6

7

2

3

8

9

0

1

4

SUDOKU

A Game for Mathematicians

FIll out the blocks so that the numbers one to nine will only appear once in each row, colum and 3x3 grid.

		9	7	3		5	2	6
		5		2		8		
6		8					4	7
				9			6	2
	4		6		3		8	
8	9		5					
2	6					1		8
		7		1		6		
9	5	1		6	4	2		